AF538314

The Archbishop's Cathedral

by Carl Sheppard

with Prolegomenon
by Thomas Steele, S.J.

a publication of the
Historical Society of New Mexico

a publication of the

Historical Society of New Mexico

First Printing 1995

Cimarron Press
Santa Fe, New Mexico U.S.A.

ISBN 0-9631401-0-8

Printed in the United States of America

Contents

Prolegomenon 4

En la Llegada 5

I. A New Bishop; A New Sanctuary 8

II. Inspiration and Influences 19

III. Continuance 35

Appendix A 48

Appendix B 50

List of Illustrations 54

Index 58

ARCHBISHOP J.B. LAMY
· 1850-1888 ·

figs. 1, 2. In 1915, Miguel Chaves donated the bronze statue of Archbishop Lamy which still stands outside Lamy's cathedral in Santa Fe. It was formally dedicated in lengthy and impressive ceremonies on Sunday 23 May. Invited orator Nestor Montoya, politician and editor of Albuquerque's La Bandera Americana, *had often used Rómulo Ribera's poetry in his paper, and since a Ribera poem written some months earlier was so pertinent to the occasion, Montoya ran it in* La Bandera Americana *and then used it to conclude his stirring address.*

PROLEGOMENON

José Rómulo Ribera (c. 1848-1917) attended the seminary and was ordained, but he left the priesthood to become a teacher; he dabbled in politics and published a lot of poetry in newspapers. In 1914, he wrote this very sophisticated poem which Nestor Montoya read the next year at the dedication of Miguel Chaves' bronze statue of Archbishop Lamy that stands in front of the Santa Fe Cathedral, and Montoya printed it in the Albuquerque weekly *La Bandera Americana*. Probably with help from Demetrio Pérez' manuscript account of the event, Ribera's heroic Lamy, the archetypal man on horseback, symbolizes Christ entering the Jerusalem temple as triumphant Yahweh Sabaoth, as arriving pilgrim, and as sacrificial victim. Hence the poem implies the dawning of linear, rational, masculine, reflective consciousness and the eclipse of tribal and peasant ways of thinking ("*genízaro* awareness"); Nuevomejicano culture here abases itself before French clerical culture. Furthermore, José Rómulo Ribera's "En la Llegada" dovetails perfectly with Father William Howlett's admiring treatment of Lamy in his 1908 *Life of Bishop Machebeuf*, sculptor J. Jusko's statue, and Willa Cather's aesthetic Jean Baptiste Latour in her 1927 novel *Death comes to the Archbishop.*

Thomas Steele, S.J.

En La LLegada

On the Entrance of His Illustrious Lordship
Don Jean Baptiste Lamy into Sante Fe

¡Qué éntusiasmo! ¡qué alegría!
¡qué júbilo! ¡qué alborozo!
¡ya llegó su Señoría!
¡ya vino el pastor piadoso!

De gala está Santa Fé,
arcos de triunfo doquiera,
la gente forma una hilera
y arrodillada se vé,
la razón yo bien lo sé,
la sabe el pueblo gustoso
y en arranque tumultuoso
repite como a porfía:
¡ya llegó su Señoría!
¡ya vino el pastor piadoso!

Las campanas, imitando
el júbilo popular,
en fiesta tan singular
todas están repicando.
Melodiosas anunciando
que unprelado muy virtuoso
humilde, santo, ejemploso
a la diócesis venía:
¡ya llegó su Señoría!
¡ya vino el pastor piadoso!

What enthusiasm, what happiness,
What jubilee, what celebration!
Now his Lordship entered,
The holy pastor has arrived!

Santa Fe is gaily adorned,
Triumphal arches everywhere
The people form a line
And kneel in reverent prayer
The reason I know indeed
As do the joyful people,
And with a joyous outcry
They repeat as a refrain,
"Now his Lordship enters,
The holy pastor has arrived!"

The bells, resounding
The people's jubilee
At such a glorious fiesta,
Are all ringing,
Proclaiming in melody,
That a most virtuous prelate
Humble, holy, exemplary,
Is approaching the diocese:
Now his Lordship enters,
The holy pastor has arrived.

Gente, a caballo montada
al ilustre peregrino,
vá señalando el camino
de la ciudad a la entrada.
ya terminó la jornada
de un viaje tan azaroso;
lo aclama el clero obsequioso,
ya se oye, la vocería:
¡qué vivá su Señoría!
qué vivá el pastor piadoso!

People on horseback
Ride out to the noble traveler
Showing him the way
From the entrance to the city.
Now the journey has ended,
The trip so tiresome,
The attentive clergy acclaim him,
The loud cry is heard,
"Long live his Lordship!
Long live the holy pastor!"

Día de feliz memoria
en esa ciudad grandiosa,
la página mas hermosa
de todas las de su historia
bendito día de gloria
cuando aquel pueblo afanoso
contento y lleno de gozo
uno al otro se decía
¡ya llegó su Señoría!
¡ya vino el pastor piadoso!

Day of happy memory
For that magnificent city,
The most beautiful page
Of all its history
Blest day of glory
When those eager people,
Content and joyful,
Cried one to the other,
"Now his Lordship enters,
The holy pastor has arrived!

Un jóven alto y lozano,
de hermoso aspecto y derecho,
con una cruz sobre el pecho
y un pastoral en su mano,
saluda al pueblo cristiano,
humilde, sí, mas airoso

A young man, tall and vigorous,
Of handsome, correct appearance,
With a cross upon his breast
And pastoral ring on hand,
Greets the Christian people
Humbly but with energy

montado en corcel fogoso,

As he sits his fiery steed;

¡ya llegó su Señoría!
¡ya vino el pastor piadoso!

Now his Lordship enters,
The holy pastor has arrived!

Despues de la bienvenida
entró al templo, allí postrado,
a jesus sacramentado
le ofreció su santa vida.
A la gente alli reunida
la amonestó muy zeloso
y les prometió anhieloso
servirles de ejemplo y guia;
¡ya llegó su Señoría!
¡ya vino el pastor piadoso!

After the welcome
He entered the temple and knelt
To Jesus in the sacrament.
He offered his holy life
To the people gathered there.
He exhorted the assembled people
And earnestly promised them
To be their example and guide
Now his Lordship enters,
The holy pastor has arrived!

Asi lo hizo, pues su vida
fué ejemplar y muy virtuosa
su santa muerte preciosa,
su memoria bendecida.
Hoy la gente agradecida
recuerda aquel sueño hermoso
y aquel eco estrepitoso
de uno al otro se decia
¡ya llegó su Señoría!
¡ya vino el pastor piadoso!

Thus he did, for his life was
Exemplary and very virtuous.
His holy precious death
Makes his memory blest.
Now a thankful people
Recall that beautiful dream,
Their powerful echo
When they said to one another,
"Now his Lordship enters,
"The holy pastor has arrived!"

-José Rómulo Ribera

I. A New Bishop; a New Sanctuary

The old adobe Church of Saint Francis, the Parroquia (figs. 3-5), dominated the Santa Fe scene architecturally in 1850 at the time Bishop Jean-Baptiste Lamy (pronounced lah-me in France and lay-me in New Mexico) arrived to take up his duties. He did not like his new Cathedral. Eventually he had the church dismantled, replaced by an unusual structure that can be explained as an expression of his personal history. It became his personal monument. As a Frenchman, Lamy preferred the contemporary architecture of the Napoleonic Second Empire and had schools, dormitories, hospitals, convents all constructed in the appropriate manner of the Second Empire: relatively tall for Santa Fe, with mansard roofs and towers, built nevertheless of adobe.

Very evocative of what he accomplished in the dusty village are the structures housing the Convent of Our Lady of Light, the Loretto Chapel and the Loretto Academy (fig. 6). Except for the chapel, the buildings were built of adobe. The convent was named Our Lady of Light after the dedication of the ruined military chapel which stood on the town plaza. The nuns came from the Diocese of Louisville, Kentucky, and were of the Order of Loretto. Only the chapel now stands (fig. 7). The rest of the land is taken up by streets and a modern hotel. The Cathedral Lamy built, however, was another matter of style and construction from

fig. 3. La Parroquia [the Parish Church], Santa Fe; view from the northwest, c. 1867.

fig. 4. La Parroquia, view looking east along San Francisco Street, c. 1865.

fig. 5. La Parroquia, view from the northwest, c. 1867.

that of the Loretto buildings.

When Lamy arrived in the Territory of New Mexico, the land had been taken from Mexico only four years previously. He had to establish his independence from the Bishop of Durango in the state of Chihuahua, Mexico, and affirm his friendship with the Bishop of Cincinnati where he had been since he came to America from France in 1839. His allegiance to the Diocese of Cincinnati never lessened and he received much assistance in his work from the authorities in Ohio. Even more assistance was probably forthcoming from the Archbishop of Clermont-Ferrand in France. Lamy had been born in the region of Auvergne, south central France, and educated at Clermont. It remained a source of finances and personnel for Santa Fe.

This book is not intended to present new research for the history of the Cathedral at Santa Fe. Rather it is hoped that a new interpretation of style and symbol for the Cathedral, particularly its facade, will be demonstrated. Most of the information about the building, its architects and the sequence of construction has been taken from *Bishop Lamy's Santa Fe Cathedral* by Bruce Ellis, 1985; *Historical Sketch of the Cathedral in New Mexico*, by James H. Defouri, 1887; and *Atzlan, Legend of Montezuma*, by William G. Ritch, 1885.

Archbishop Lamy's Cathedral stands at the east end of San Francisco Street in Santa Fe. In spite of the style of its architecture, the building fits admirably into the present Santa Fe scene. This is only partially because the structure is not completed; the unfinished twin towers fortunately lack a great deal of height and consequently do not destroy the comfortable cityscape unbarred by irregular heights, pinnacles, towers, etc. The scale of the Cathedral is definitely human rather than abstract because of the size of entrances, window apertures, the location of cross mouldings, column capitals, pilasters; even more explicitly, one can determine subjectively proportions and size by the placement of steps, doors, even door knobs and come to a decision concerning scale. Almost without exception Santa Fe buildings embody the same projection of scale that appeals to the people in the town. Above all the earthtone colors of the locally quarried stone permits the French style Cathedral to fit into Santa Fe without disturbance. The stone itself comes from a site southeast of Santa Fe, which once belonged to the Archbishop. The building is, however, an anomaly.

The Cathedral itself and the personality of Jean-Baptiste Lamy have been cloaked by romanticism in recent times, as the French intrusion on the Hispanic village has faded and become legend in such presentations as *Death Comes for the Archbishop* by Willa Cather. In 1975 Paul Horgan wrote in his Pulitzer prize winning biography of Lamy:

> From childhood Jean-Baptiste Lamy, gazing from the tilled fields well to the north of Lempdes (his home), across bluing hills, to the farthest line of the land where the solitary profile of the Puy-de-Dome rose in the distance, could see between near and far the hazy cluster of the city of Clermont-Ferrand. The only constant and distinguishable features which he could pick out were the two spires of the cathedral side by side, there, at the end of the country road leading from Lempdes to the city and the world. At that angle, in certain lights they might fancifully suggest the twin spires of a mitre, such as worn by a bishop, a lord and teacher.

fig. 6. The Loretto Academy, the Loretto Chapel, and the Convent of Our Lady of Light, Santa Fe, c. 1900

fig. 7. The Loretto Chapel, facade, 1976-1977.

Emotionally provocative, perhaps, but based on an error. The cathedral had no twin spires when Lamy was at Lempdes. The present facade was not designed until 1865 by Viollet-le-Duc (fig. 8). The completed facade of the Auvergnat Cathedral possibly had some influence on Lamy but it is difficult to determine with precision what it was.

The cornerstone of the Cathedral of Saint Francis in Santa Fe was laid on July 14, 1867. It was not until 1869, however, that the craftsman-architect, Antoine Moulay and his son, Projectus, also a competent craftsman-architect, arrived in Santa Fe; Lamy had found them in Auvergne. The Moulays were from Volvic, a village not far from Riom where Lamy had been born. He brought them to the United States just before the Franco-Prussian War began in 1870. Lamy had been in Rome in October of 1869 and back in Santa Fe in June 1870. This was his second trip to Europe; the first had been taken in 1853 to Rome but he touched Clermont both coming and going. Perhaps the Moulays drew up plans for the structure based on sketches provided by Lamy at that time. It is known they drew up plans and elevations for the church.

The Moulays had to cope with foundations already in place but apparently inadequately laid down. They renewed the basis of the building and narrowed it considerably. Unfortunately, the elder Moulay lost his sight and returned to France in 1874.

There was a several year stoppage of work at the Cathedral of Santa Fe and the architects were free to work elsewhere. They were hired in 1874 by the Sisters of Loretto to work on the Loretto Chapel. That building developed as an excellent example of mid-thirteenth century Gothic, one

fig. 8. Project for the facade of the Cathedral of Clermont-Ferrand, Violet-le-duc.

of the earliest Gothic Revival structures west of the Mississippi, and perhaps influenced by Viollet-le-Duc's design for Clermont-Ferrand. In any event, the chapel recalls palace architecture of the Ile-de-France and has no connection with Lamy's Cathedral.

On February 12, 1874, Lamy was promoted to be Archbishop. That year he returned to France for funds and assistance. In 1878, a new set of plans was drawn up by Francois Mallet, who came to Santa Fe via San Francisco. By March of 1879, Mallet had submitted drawings for the facade, other elevations, and plans for the Cathedral. Unfortunately, he was shot to death by the Archbishop's nephew in September of that year. The young Lamy had been infuriated by the attentions paid to his young wife by the architect. He was judicially condemned but a few days later freed on grounds of temporary insanity.

Eventually, in 1882, the firm of Monier and Machebeuf was given the contract to complete the Cathedral and oversee the demolition of the adobe Parroquia, around and over which the new building was being constructed. A stereoptical view taken in 1881 (fig. 9), shows the roof of the old church to the west with the great gap between its outer wall and the wall of the new construction. The old roof was, of course, going to be used as scaffolding for the new roof. The Archbishop died in 1888 before his Cathedral was finished; but, he was able enjoy the completed nave.

There is no reason to doubt the drawings of Mallet, utilizing the construction accomplished by the Moulays, account for the present design of the Cathedral. Examination of the fabric of the church suggests, along with photographs, that the present appearance of the Cathedral had been established from the start in 1870. Stereopticon views (figs. 10-12) in 1880 and 1881 indicate as much. The earlier one shows the Cathedral with the facade almost up to the first level of the towers and the base of the rose window. The lateral side is finished to above the level of the aisle windows. Even with this much progress, however, the original western towers still rise above the new construction and show the facade as an independent construction in front of the old church.

The second stereopticon shows the north tower well into its second stage, little more has been accomplished for the rose window and the south tower seem to be at the same level. These two views, nevertheless, indicate that the design of the facade had been established from the beginning no matter the changes of finance or designers. From the inception, Lamy's Cathedral had twin facade towers, Romanesque detailing over the lowest section, and a simple rose window above. In spite of the changes of contractors, architects, the hiatus in activity and the slowness caused by lack of funds, the Cathedral achieved the essential design established in the early 1870's.

In April, 1884, the Archbishop was given a coadjutor, and in July, 1885, Lamy retired. The Cathedral bell was blessed on 7 March, 1886. Lamy died in 1888. The present condition of the east end of the church, the sanctuary, transepts and contiguous chapels, was not completed until 1967. Our purpose is to discuss that design and the present appearance of the church.

fig. 9. Cathedral of St. Francis, Santa Fe, 1880 , view showing the roof and the south wall of the nave of the Parroquia, paralleled by the new stone construction of the exterior south wall.

fig. 10. Cathedral of St. Francis, Santa Fe, c. 1880, view showing construction of the Cathedral around the Parroquia, whose facade towers still emerge at the west.

fig. 11. Cathedral of St. Francis, Santa Fe, c. 1881, view showing construction of the new building up to the level of the first story of the facade.

fig. 12. The clock of La Parroquia as the new Cathedral rises around it, c. 1880.

fig. 13. Cathedral of St. Francis, Santa Fe, west facade, 1992.

II. Inspiration and Influences

At present the Cathedral (fig. 13) passes in most discussions as Romanesque as in the guide, *New Mexico Architecture*, where it is treated as Romanesque Revival. Among the first mentions of the style of the Cathedral is that of William Ritch in 1885. He calls the building Roman Byzantium. Two years later James Defouri designates it as Roman Style in referring to the vaults of the nave. The term "Romanesque" became current in France during the second decade of the nineteenth century. It was the last of the designations of the great European styles to gain currency. The Romanesque Revival did not come about until some sixty years later through the work of H.H. Richardson in New England, the only phenomenon of that type to originate in the United States. Lamy's facade owes nothing to Richardson. His design for a facade is earlier than any of the Revival on the East Coast. Its source is outside the mainstream of American architecture. It was the archbishop's own invention. It reflects the Romanesque of Auvergne. I say reflects because it is not a precise evocation of the Romanesque buildings in the region of Clermont, the homeland of the Bishop. Indeed, only the lowest division of the facade can be called Romanesque, except for the capitals of the second floor of the towers.

Lamy did incorporate enough of the Auvergnat Romanesque for his facade to pass as dependent on that

fig. 14. Cathedral of St. Francis, Santa Fe, west facade, central portal, 1993.

fig. 15. Church of Notre Dame, Puy-de-Dome, France, side portal with polychromy.

style. Most noticeable is the polychromy of the lower part of the church (fig. 14). Reddish-purple stones are interspersed by whitish ones for the arches of the main entrance and the arches over the blind openings of the lower level of the towers.

The use of polychromy was widespread around Clermont as in a portal of the facade of Notre Dame, Puy-de-Dome (fig. 15), or the east end of Notre Dame-du-Port, Clermont-Ferrand, itself. The polychromed archivolts plus the field of red stone behind and above the main entrance at Santa Fe attest to Lamy's interest in maintaining his connection with the architecture of his homeland. Not only do details such as the type of capitals (fig. 16) for all the columns but other architectural features such as portal and window openings show a relation to the architecture of twelfth century Auvergne. Unfortunately for a neat analysis the rest of the facade has no relation to any Romanesque buildings anywhere. Nevertheless, the lowest section of the facade must have symbolized for Lamy the places he was born and trained-- the basis of his life and career.

The corner towers of the facade were certainly decided upon from the beginning of the construction by the Moulays. No indication of an alteration to the structure, either from the source materials or from surface analysis suggests otherwise. There is nothing unusual about their appearance in the design at Santa Fe, except that towers at the corners are not usual in Auvergne. Rather they are placed on the center axis. However, by the thirteenth century, Gothic style twin towered facades were common throughout France. Viollet-le-Duc's project for Clermont might have had some influence, too. Perhaps the Bishop was merely recalling his general patrimony.

Fray Angelico Chavez suggests, however, the towers

fig. 16. Cathedral of St. Francis, Santa Fe, south side, south tower, first floor, Romanesque Revival capitals,. Photograph 1993.

fig. 17. Cathedral of Chihuahua, facade.

fig. 18. Cathedral of St. Francis, Santa Fe, west facade, detail of north tower base showing Ionic capitals. Photograph, 1993.

of the Cathedral of Chihuahua (fig. 17). Unfortunately, the facade of the Cathedral of Chihuahua is executed in a fine baroque manner. Its handsome three staged rectangular towers may have been caught Fray Chavez' attention with their verticality, but there the similarity ends to the octagonal spires of Lamy's design.

The selection of the debased Ionic Order (fig. 18) for each stage of the towers is nevertheless inexplicable to me. I can give no reason for their grossness. The scrolls have been reduced to mere channels grooved in the surfaces and the bolsters appear as large mouldings. Normally a corner Ionic capital is adjusted so the ends of the volutes project at 45° at each corner and eliminate the bolsters. Here they are allowed to remain. The reduced three-dimensionality of the capitals and their inadequate rendering (they can't even be called provincial or archaic) do not accord with any other feature of the facade.

In 1885, the text of W.G. Ritch's *Aztlan, Legend of Montezuma* published a line cut (fig. 19) of the Cathedral of San Francisco. The full page illustration was signed by the Mills Engineering Company of Denver. It is the only evidence of what the completed towers of the church would have looked like. Above the first octagonal stage rise three windowed storeys, capped by a low dome. The dome over the crossing appears as it was originally planned but also was never erected. The line cut seems to give an accurate image of the Cathedral as it was thought of in 1885. As mentioned, the first story of the illustration has many reminiscences of twelfth century Auvergne but what about the towers! The three stages merely repeat the lowest octagonal shape becoming smaller at each level. This is not a Romanesque design nor a Gothic one. Where did the

fig. 19. Cathedral of St. Francis, Santa Fe, line-cut showing proposed but never completed towers, 1885.

Bishop and his architect get the idea for this particular design? It is not Auvergnat; it is not medieval; it is not French.

The towers do not represent the Bishop's homeland nor do they replicate any Italian monument he may have seen during his travels at Rome, Florence, Milan, Genoa, etc. The types close to the Santa Fe towers are to be found in eighteenth century neoclassic churches of England but Lamy had never been there. The closest parallel I have found is the tower dominating the Cathedral of St. Peter-in-Chains, Cincinnati, (fig. 20) the church in which Lamy was made a bishop and on which he was dependant for his early missionary years in Ohio and Kentucky. The design at Cincinnati is much more sophisticated than that possibly drawn up for Santa Fe. The stepped octagons and the open columned stages do give semblance to the two buildings. If Cincinnati was the source for the Santa Fe towers Lamy was probably symbolizing his connection with his first home in America from which he was sent out to the new Territories of the West.

The third possible symbol involved in the design of the facade consists of the middle section of the facade above the main portal. A large rectangle punctuated by a handsome rose window and a strongly marked triangle with a small oculus have no stylistic connection with the Romanesque lower part nor the post-renaissance towers. Except for the mouldings marking the triangle the rest belongs to the early Gothic mode. What could be the explanation for this aberration, the introduction of early Gothic elements? The simplicity of the forms, the inclusion of stained

fig. 20. Cathedral of Saint-Peter-in-Chains, Cincinnati.

fig. 21. Church of San Francesco, Assisi, west facade.

glass do recall one of the most famous churches built in the early thirteenth century, St. Francis at Assisi (fig. 21), the first church to honor the newly consecrated Saint. Since the Cathedral at Santa Fe was dedicated to Saint Francis, and since Lamy certainly had visited Assisi during his many trips to Italy, what could be more appropriate for Santa Fe than a reference to the great Franciscan monastic church?

I have said very little about the nave (fig. 22) of Lamy's church because it does not vary much from a twelfth or thirteenth century church interior of French origin. The nave elevation is unlike any prototype in Auvergne, however. The churches there are very dark because they are covered by barrel vaults and have a two part elevation of arcade and gallery without a clerestory. the elevation at Santa Fe is two-part also but has a clerestory and no gallery. The interior is consequently well lit. The nave and side aisles are covered by domed cross and groin vaults made of light tufa stone, separated by transverse ribs, a solution unusual in central France but not uncommon elsewhere. The capitals of the columns of the nave and the corbels of the clerestory are made of metal, probably cast-iron, and were ordered from a company in St. Louis specializing in architectural details.

Whether or not any of these observations is correct, it is certainly interesting to provide symbolic interpretations for the Cathedral facade of Santa Fe and to explain partially the strangeness of the design. Although the type of evidence is not very strong for the conclusions I have drawn, it seems more than possible that Bishop Lamy did select parts of his Cathedral facade to symbolize his career, his indebtedness to others and to Saint Francis.

fig. 22. Cathedral of St. Francis, Santa Fe, interior, nave towards crossing, 1981.

III. Continuance

In 1986, the interior of the Cathedral underwent considerable refurbishment. At the time of the original consecration under Archbishop Lamy the nave ended at the two heavy columns closing it to the east. Curtains were slung across the space to hide the old sanctuary and chapels. The interior was unpainted and left rather white, the natural color of the materials used. Harsh light was mitigated through the installation of colored glass windows made by an atelier at Clermont-Ferrand, France, representing ten of the twelve Apostles. The windows for the other two Apostles were probably placed on either side of the sanctuary. The windows of the clerestory now carry the coats of arms of the sequence of the Archbishops of Santa Fe. Further changes have been made to the interior since Lamy completed his nave.

Serious repairs were undertaken in 1935, '39, and '40 by the architect John Gaw Meem (fig.23). In his biography of Meem, Bainbridge Bunting reported the nave vaults were "reinforced by pouring concrete arches above the ribs and tying these with long rods drilled through the stone ribs to curved plates of steel fitted to the intradosses of the old ribs. An elaborate series of metal tie rods one on each side of every transverse rib, was provided for the nave and side aisles."

In 1940 new and deeper footings for all of the piers were provided and the foundations of walls and buttresses

fig. 23. Cathedral of St. Francis, Santa Fe, south side of nave, under reconstruction, 1939-1940.

fig. 24. Cathedral of St. Francis, Santa Fe, interior, nave, service c. 1948.

fig. 25. Cathedral of St. Francis, Santa Fe, Chapel of La Conquistadora .

were encased in concrete. As a result of decisions made at Vatican Council II, the sanctuary of the cathedral was redone by architect Urban Widner and completed in 1967-68 (fig. 24). For the Cathedral centenary celebration the interior was painted white with appropriate decorative stencils in green, gold and brown placed on the nave and aisle column capitals, on mouldings, and particularly along the underside of the arches and the groins of the vaults, giving the effect of ribs.

The Chapel of La Conquistadora (fig. 25), or as she has recently been renamed, Our Lady of Peace, whose foundations go back to the early eighteenth century, adjoins the sanctuary to the north. It was restored by 1954, in celebration of the Marian Year. The Chapel is constructed of adobes and escaped the construction of Lamy's Cathedral as well as all subsequent restorations and refurbishment. It now appears as a representation of colonial New Mexico, as indeed it is. The statue of Our Lady is considered to be the oldest devotional image of the Virgin in the United States. She was brought to Santa Fe in 1625; escaped south at the time of the native revolt in 1680 and returned to stay in 1692. The Chapel gives the effect of an authentic eighteenth century sanctuary.

The huge construction closing the east wall of the sanctuary is a most recent addition to the Cathedral. The reredos (fig. 26) contains thirteen panels, each dedicated to a religious figure involved in some way with worship in the Southwest. It includes a carved figure of Saint Francis and above him a painting of the great Mexican interpretation of the Virgin Mary as Our Lady of Guadalupe, at the apex of the screen. (See Appendix A for details.)

The bronze doors (fig. 27) of the Cathedral, designed and executed by architect and sculptor Donna Quasthoff, were installed in 1986. Their sixteen panels tell the story of the Catholic religion in New Mexico ending with the construction of the Cathedral and the completion of the great reredos. (See Appendix B for descriptions.)

In his 1993 *Sanctuaries of Spanish New Mexico,* Marc Treib gave his opinion of Lamy's Cathedral: "Today it is a handsome church with little of particular aesthetic note." Of course, Treib wrote in the context of Spanish New Mexico. The facade of the Cathedral of New Mexico belongs to a different order. It is clearly not Spanish, nor even very French. It is made from different styles and sources. It definitely is a unique design, and almost an autobiography. It is a personal revelation that dominates the architecture of modern Santa Fe, and one of the very few buildings anywhere to present the personality of its patron.

fig. 26. Cathedral of St. Francis, Santa Fe, sanctuary reredos, Robert Lentz, artist..

Appendix A

The Sanctuary Reredos

Saints of the Americas

Top Row from left to right
St. Philip of Jesus, St. Rose of Lima; Our Lady of Guadalupe; St. Martin de Porres, St. Francis Solano.

Second Row
St. John Neumann, St. Elizabeth Seton, St. Francis of Assisi, St. Francis Cabrini, St. Peter Claver.

Third Row
Bl. Katherine Drexel, St. Isaac Jogues, Bl. Kateri Tekakwitha, Bl. Junipera Serra, St. Miguel Febres Cordero.

fig. 27. Cathedral of St. Francis, Santa Fe, west facade. Central portal, bronze doors. Donna Quasthoff, sculptor, 1986.

Appendix B

Cathedral of St. Francis, Santa Fe, Bronze Doors

Panel 1. In 1539, Fray Marcos de Niza first sighted the Zuni Pueblos from afar, and named the whole region "The Kingdom of St. Francis."

Panel 2. In 1583, three friars came, but were slain by the Indians of the Middle Rio Grande valley. But it is they who gave the name NEW MEXICO to the region.

Panel 3. In 1598, at San Juan de los Caballeros, Don Juan de Oñate founded the first Spanish Colony and Franciscan Mission.

Panel 4. In 1610*, Santa Fe was founded as the Capital of a promising "Kingdom of New Mexico." Here a small church was built as the very first parish under the title of Our Lady of the Assumption.

Panel 5. In 1625, Fr. Alonso de Benavides brought with him by caravan from the city of Mexico, along with other articles for the parish church of the Assumption, a pretty statue of our Lady. Fr. Benavides, a Franciscan appointed to preside over the missions in New Mexico, subsequently tore down the small parish church and built a larger church for the statue which soon became "La Conquistadora."

Panel 6. In 1680, the Indian pueblos rebelled, killing 21 friars and some settlers. The Santa Fe parish was burned while the settlers fled down to El Paso del Norte with their dear Conquistadora.

Panel 7. In 1693, after the reconquest of Santa Fe, General Don Diego de Vargas in a ceremony conducted on the plaza of Santa Fe, solemnly turned the missions over to the Fathers, and the city to its mayor and council.

Panel 8. In 1730, Bishop Benito Crespo from New Spain appointed a secular priest, Don Santiago Roybal, as his resident vicar in Santa Fe. With Bishop Crespo's arrival in Santa Fe, the parish church witnessed its very first episcopal ceremonial. Vicar Roybal was one of the earliest native-born priests of what is now the continental United States.

Panel 9. In 1846, General Stephen Watts Kearney took Santa Fe and New Mexico for the U.S.A. Although not a Catholic, he attended Mass with his Catholic men following their arrival. The Vicar was Juan Felipe Ortiz.

Panel 10. In 1850, Santa Fe was made a bishopric. Bishop Lamy arrived a year later and chose the parish church as his Cathedral, also choosing St. Francis as the patron saint of the new diocese. Recognizing the need for Catholic education, Bishop Lamy in 1852 escorted from their convent in Kentucky six Sisters of Loretto to New Mexico.

Panel 11. In 1869, Bishop Lamy laid the cornerstone for his stone Cathedral, the walls and columns to rise around the old adobe church, which continued in use. By this time he had brought the Sisters of Charity and the Christian Brothers to New Mexico.

Panel 12. In 1875, Santa Fe was elevated to an Archdiocese. By 1880, the roof and walls of the Old Parroquia can still be seen within the rising new walls of St. Francis Cathedral. In the background, Lamy and the architect discuss the plans while the stone masons are seen working in the foreground.

Panel 13. In 1886, the main nave was completed enough to allow its first use when Lamy blessed the structure and sang the first Mass.

Panel 14. In 1912, New Mexico became a State of the Union and in 1915, three years later, Governor William C. McDonald and Archbishop John Baptist Pitaval dedicated the Lamy statue in front of the Cathedral. Mrs. Miguel Chavez and J.B. Lamy (nephew) can be seen unveiling the American flag from the statue.

Panel 15. In 1954, the U.S. Catholics celebrated a Marian Year. This brought on the Episcopal Coronation of La Con quistadora as the oldest Marian statue of Mary in the country. Six years later, in 1960, the Apostolic Delegate, Archbishop Egidio Vagnozzi, performed a similar Papal

Coronation. Archbishop Byrne is standing to the left of La Conquistadora.

Panel 16. In 1986, the Apostolic Delegate, Archbishop Pio Laghi, assisted by Archbishop Robert F. Sanchez and 21 other Bishops, celebrated the Centenary of the Cathedral's blessing by her first Archbishop with the Liturgy and consecration of a new altar. This scene portrays the Our Father signed in Tewa by an Indian woman.

The doors were cast and assembled at Shidoni Foundry, north of Santa Fe.

*Recent reseach may suggest that Santa Fe was actually established in 1607.

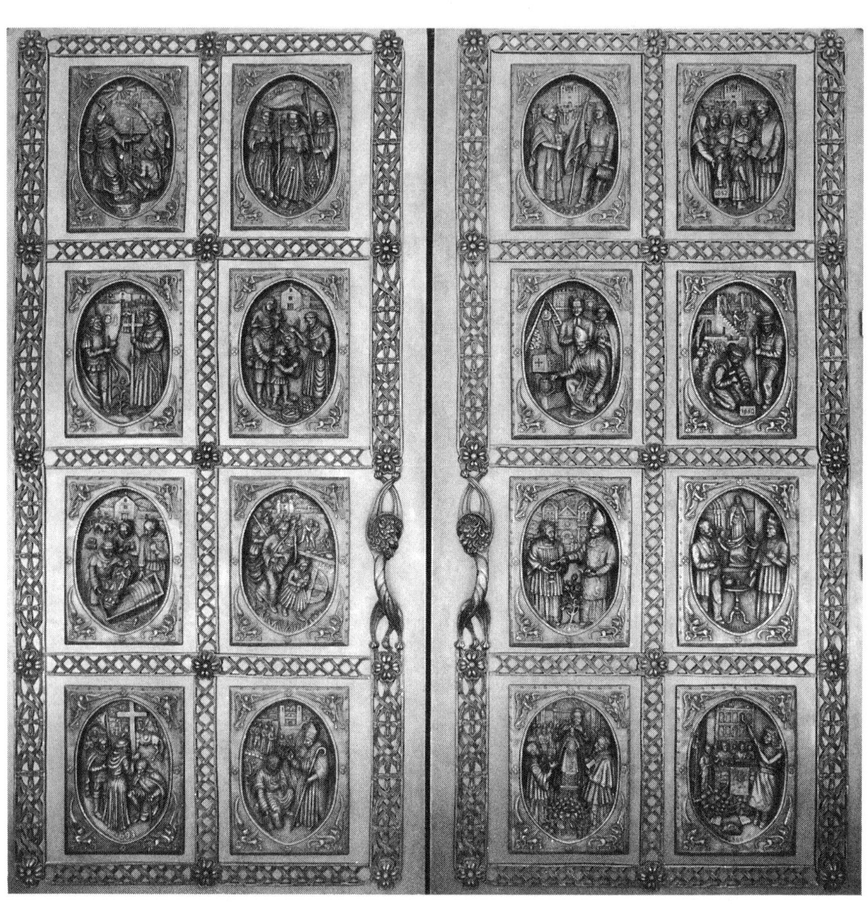

fig. 28. Cathedral of St. Francis, Santa Fe, bronze doors.

List of Illustrations

Fig. 1. Bronze statue of Archbishop Jean-Baptiste Lamy, life size, by J. Jusko, 1915. Museum of New Mexico Neg. #74067. 2

Fig. 2. Dedication of statue in honor of Archbishop Lamy, 23 May 1915, MNM Neg.# 74067. 3

Fig. 3. La Parroquia (the Parish Church), Santa Fe, view from the northwest, c. 1867. MNM Neg. #55484. 10

Fig. 4. La Parroquia, view along San Francisco Street, c. 1865. MNM Neg. #11330. 11

Fig. 5. La Parroquia, view from the northwest, c. 1867. Photo by Nicholas Brown, MNM Neg. # 55484. 12

Fig. 6. The Loretto Academy, the Loretto Chapel and the Convent of Our Lady of Light, Santa Fe, c. 1900. Photo by John C. Gullette, MNM Neg. # 13262. 15

Fig. 7. The Loretto Chapel facade, 1976-77. Photo by Arthur Taylor, MNM Neg. #117110. 16

Fig. 8. Project for the facade of the Cathedral of Clermont-Ferrand, Violet-le-Duc, courtesy of the Caisse Nationale des Monuments Historiques. 18

Fig. 9. Cathedral of St. Francis, Santa Fe, 1880, view showing the roof and the south wall of the nave of the Parroquia. Photo by Ben Wittick, El Paso Centennial Museum, University of Texas at El Paso, MNM Neg. #58401. 21

Fig. 10. Cathedral of St. Francis, Santa Fe, c. 1880, view showing construction of the Cathedral around the Parroquia. Photo by George C. Bennett, MNM Neg. #127377. 22

Fig. 11. Cathedral of St. Francis, Santa Fe, c. 1881, view showing construction. Photo by Ben Wittick, El Paso Centennial Museum, UTEP, MNM Neg. #58399. 23

Fig. 12. The clock of La Parroquia, c. 1880. Photo by Ben Wittick, MNM Neg. # 149374. 24

Fig. 13. Cathedral of Santa Fe, west facade, 1992. 25

Fig. 14. Cathedral of St. Francis, Santa Fe, west facade, central portal. Photo by Agnesa Reeve, 1993. 28

Fig. 15. Church of Notre Dame, Puy-de-Dome, France. 29

Fig. 16. Cathedral of St. Francis, Santa Fe, south side, south tower. Photo by Agnesa Reeve, 1993. 31

Fig. 17. Cathedral of Chihuahua, Mexico, c. 1883. Photo by William Henry Jackson, MNM Neg. #74696. 32

Fig. 18. Cathedral of St. Francis, Santa Fe, detail of north tower base. Photo by Agnesa Reeve, 1993. 33

Fig. 19. Cathedral of San Francis, Santa Fe, line cut, 1885, Mills Engineering Co. 35

Fig. 21. Church of San Francesco, Assisi, west facade. 38

Fig. 22. Cathedral of St. Francis, Santa Fe, interior. 1981. Photo by Marc Treib, MNM Neg. #99772. 40

Fig. 23. Cathedral of St. Francis, Santa Fe, interior under reconstruction., 1939-40. Photo by Margaret McKittrick, MNM Neg. #30681. 42

Fig. 24. Cathedral of St. Francis, Santa Fe, interior during service, c. 1948. Photo by Robert H. Martin, MNM Neg. #41299. 43

Fig. 25. Cathedral of St. Francis, Santa Fe, Chapel of La Conquistadora, 1975. Photo by Robert Brewer, MNM Neg. #65143. 44

Fig. 26. Cathedral of St. Francis, Santa Fe, the sanctuary reredos. Photo by Ed. Taylor. 47

Fig. 27. Cathedral of St. Francis, Santa Fe, west facade, central portal, bronze doors, Donna Quasthoff, sculptor, 1986. 49

Fig. 28. Cathedral of St. Francis, Santa Fe, bronze doors. Photo by Hope A. Curtis. 53

Index

A

adobe 9, 19, 45, 48
Archbishop 19. *See also* Jean-Baptiste Lamy; death of 19; Lamy promoted to 19
architects 13, 17, 45
Assisi 39
Auvergnat Cathedral 17
Auvergne 13, 17, 27, 30, 34, 39
Aztlan, Legend of Montezuma 13, 34

B

baroque 34
bronze doors 45, 46
Bunting, Bainbridge 41

C

capitals 30, 31, 33, 34, 39, 45
Cathedral of Chihuahua 34
Cathedral of San Francisco 34
Cathedral of St. Peter-in-Chains 36. *See also* Cincinnati
Cather, Willa 4, 14
Chapel of La Conquistadora 45. *See also* La Conquistadora
Chaves, Miguel 3, 4
Chavez, Fray Angelico 30
Chihuahua 13, 34
Cincinnati 13, 36, 37, 52
Clermont-Ferrand 13, 14, 19, 30, 41
columns 30, 41
Convent of Our Lady of Light 51

D

Death Comes for the Archbishop. 4, 14
Defouri, James H. 13, 27
dome 34
Durango 13

E

Ellis, Bruce 13

F

facade 13, 20, 30, 34, 36, 39
France 9, 13, 17, 19, 27, 30, 39
Franciscan 39, 47

G

Gothic 34, 36
Gothic Revival 19, 30

H

Horgan, Paul 14

I

Ionic Order 34

J

Jean-Baptiste Lamy *See also* Archbishop; 9, 14, 51; arrival in New Mexico 13; finds architects 17; symbolized his career 39; travels in Europe 17, 36
Jusko, J. 4

L

La Bandera Americana 3, 4
La Conquistadora 47. *See also* Conquistadora
Life of Bishop Machebeuf 4
Loretto Academy 9, 51

Loretto Chapel 9, 16, 17, 51
Louisville, Kentucky 9

M

Mallet, Francois 19
Meem, John Gaw 41
Monier and Machebeuf 19
Montoya, Nestor 3, 4
Moulay, Antoine 17
Moulays 19, 30
Mouley, Projectus 17

N

nave 19, 27, 39, 41, 45
New Mexico Architecture 27

O

Order of Loretto 9
Our Lady. *See* La Conquistadora
Our Lady of Light 9, 51
Our Lady of Peace 45

P

Parroquia 9, 10, 19, 21, 22, 24, 48, 51, 52
polychromy 28, 29, 30
Puy-de-Dome 14, 30

Q

Quasthoff, Donna 45

R

reredos 45, 47, 48
Ribera, Rómulo 4
Ribera, Rómulo 3
Richardson, H.H. 27
Ritch, William G. 13, 27

Romanesque 20, 27, 30, 34, 36
Romanesque Revival 31
roof 19
rose window 20, 36

S

scale 13, 14
Second Empire 9
St. Francis of Assisi 39
Steele, Thomas, S.J. 4

T

tone 14, 39
towers 9, 13, 20, 27, 30, 34, 36

V

Vatican Council II 45
vaults 27, 39, 41, 45
Viollet-le-Duc 17, 19, 30

W

Widner, Urban 45
windows 41